S0-DQZ-733

CENTER STAGE

BRUCE SPRINGSTEEN

By
Teresa Koenig

Edited By
Dr. Howard Schroeder
Professor in Reading and Language Arts
Dept. of Elementary Education
Mankato State University

Produced & Designed By
Baker Street Productions, Ltd.

CRESTWOOD HOUSE

Mankato, Minnesota
U.S.A.

LIBRARY OF CONGRESS CATALOGING IN PUBLICATION DATA

Koenig, Teresa.
  Bruce Springsteen

(Center stage)
SUMMARY: A brief biography of one of America's leading rock stars, who writes his own music about real problems of people.
  1. Springsteen, Bruce—Juvenile literature. 2. Rock musicians—United States—Biography—Juvenile Literature. [1. Springsteen, Bruce. 2. Musicians] I. Schroeder, Howard. II.Title. III. Series.
ML3930.S72K6   1986   784.5'4'00924 [B]   86-8961
ISBN 0-89686-303-4

**International Standard
Book Number:
0-89686-303-4**

**Library of Congress
Catalog Card Number:
86-8961**

ILLUSTRATION CREDITS:

Cover: Wide World Photos
B. Cochran/LGI: 5
Nick Elgar/LGI: 6-7, 28
Lynn Goldsmith/LGI: 8, 14, 18, 21
Wide World Photos: 13, 27, 30-31
Joe Giron/LGI: 17
George Bilyk/LGI: 22
Chuck Jackson/LGI: 25
Fabio Nosotti/LGI: 32

CRESTWOOD HOUSE
Hwy. 66 South, Box 3427
Mankato, MN 56002-3427
507-388-1616

TABLE
OF
CONTENTS

INTRODUCTION

"The luckiest man in the world"

In October, 1985, at the Los Angeles Coliseum, Bruce Springsteen ended his Born In The USA concert tour by saying, "It's been the greatest year of my life. And I want to thank you for making me feel like the luckiest man in the world."

Why does Bruce feel so lucky? He knows that he has made it through some pretty rough times. Growing up was often a struggle. But he never gave up or gave in. He picked a dream—to become a rock 'n' roll musician—and made it come true. His road to success has been long and not always smooth. Bruce also knows that the lucky feeling comes partly from his fans. He works hard and really cares about his audiences.

His 1984-'85 concert tour was his biggest ever. Over five million people paid almost ninety million dollars at the box office for a rare rock 'n' roll experience.

When Bruce Springsteen comes to town, he brings excitement with him. In Washington, D.C., the telephone system broke down for a day, this past year, when

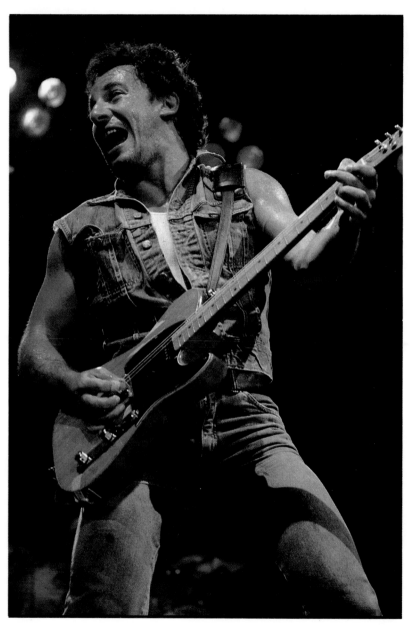

Bruce Springsteen brings excitement to each of his concerts.

his concert was announced. There were so many fans calling to buy tickets that the phone circuits were jammed from Virginia to New Jersey. A special computer system had to be used by the Illinois Bell Telephone Company when his concert tickets went on sale in the Midwest. This computer system is usually used only for towns that have been hit by a tornado.

Springsteen tickets often sell out in a matter of hours. Fans have been known to drive or fly hundreds of miles just for one night's performance. They wear 'Bruce Springsteen' T-shirts and chant his name, "Bruuuuuuce,

Bruce and his band in concert in Meadowlands, New Jersey.

Bruuuuuce, Bruuuuuuce," while waiting for him to come on stage.

Why is Bruce Springsteen so special to these people? "He's the kind of guy who makes you feel that if you were stranded after the concert, he'd take you home in his pickup truck," one fan explains. Others feel Bruce really understands and knows what they are feeling. He makes them feel that, if he can do it, they can do it. That means anything people really want, they can make happen. Bruce Springsteen has that special talent that makes people believe in themselves.

CHAPTER ONE

A rock 'n' roll dream

Bruce Frederick Springsteen was born on September 23, 1949, in Freehold, New Jersey. He was the first of three children for Douglas and Adele Springsteen.

Life was not very easy for their growing family. Bruce's mother worked as a secretary. His father, Douglas, had many jobs. He worked in a nearby factory for a while. Then he worked as a prison guard and, later, as a bus driver. Bruce watched his father struggle with disappointment. He loved his father, but Bruce wanted his own life to be different.

Bruce, second from left, wanted his life to be different.

Music was the answer for Bruce. In fact, he can remember the exact moment he decided to become a musician. In 1957, Elvis Presley introduced rock 'n' roll to the American public on the Ed Sullivan television show. Bruce was very excited by Elvis' singing and guitar playing. He knew that was what he wanted to do.

But first, he had to get a guitar. His mother bought one for him the very next day, but she insisted that he take lessons too. Bruce hated guitar lessons! So, the newly purchased guitar was soon put away and forgotten.

It was not until Bruce was a student at Freehold Regional High School in the early 1960's, that his dream of becoming a rock 'n' roll musician took hold again. Bruce was inspired by the British rock group called the Beatles. This time he bought his own guitar from a local pawn shop for $18.00 (US). Bruce Springsteen was on his way.

Practice makes perfect

As a teenager, Bruce was a loner. Before rock 'n' roll, he admits, ''I didn't have a purpose. I tried to play football and baseball and all those things. Music gave me something. It was a reason to live.'' Every day Bruce sat alone in his room listening to records and the radio for hours. He taught himself to play the guitar by imitating the songs he heard.

Years later from the concert stage, Bruce tells his fans that, "When I was first playing, I always remember my father sticking his head in the door and saying, 'turn down that guitar, turn down that radio, turn down that record.' It was always turn it down, turn it down, turn it down."

But in 1964, he was just learning how to play. Bruce's list of heroes grew to include not only Elvis and the Beatles, but also the Rolling Stones, Roy Orbison, and Gary U.S. Bonds. To be like them, he knew he had to practice a lot and practice alone. There was no time for anything else. He became totally dedicated to his music. So much time on his own also helped him to develop a strong, independent spirit.

His hard work paid off. Bruce was asked to join a local band called the Castiles. He was fifteen years old. The five Castiles performed all over New Jersey. They played at supermarket openings, junior high school dances, roller rinks, and local clubs. By the time they were booked into New York City's Cafe Wha, Bruce had started singing as well as playing guitar. He discovered that he liked singing just as much as playing.

Greetings from Asbury Park, N.J.

Only two years out of high school, Bruce had to make an important decision. His parents and two sisters were moving to California, three thousand miles away. Determined to become a professional musician, Bruce decided to stay behind. He moved eighteen miles away to Asbury Park, New Jersey, which would become an important part of Bruce's world.

After awhile, Bruce left the Castiles. He started many of his own bands. Earth, Child, Steel Mill, and Dr. Zoom and the Sonic Boom were a few of the names he chose for his bands. Each time he changed groups, it was because he wanted to improve his playing and try new styles of music.

During this time, Bruce began writing his own songs. Sometimes he would write a new song every day. His bandmembers often took jobs during the day to support themselves. Bruce's dedication to his music had not changed. He wrote songs during the day, and played with the bands at night. He lived on the little money that he made from playing in the local music clubs.

His composing, guitar playing, and singing were getting better and better. Loyal fans began to follow his progress. But something was missing. Bruce wanted more. The next step for him had to be a recording contract with a major record company. Bruce tried to

11

get a contract on his own and failed. He needed help. Early in 1972, Mike Appel and Jim Cretecos saw him perform and were impressed. They agreed to manage Bruce and help him get a record deal.

His break came a few short months later. On May 3, 1972, Bruce had an audition with John Hammond of Columbia/CBS Records. Hammond was the man who gave folksinger, Bob Dylan, a recording contract. He agreed to see Bruce, but only for fifteen minutes. Nervous, but eager to show he had talent, Bruce quickly sang his best songs. Hammond's decision was easy. He recognized talent. Bruce left the audition with what he wanted most—a chance to put his songs on a record album.

In three short weeks his first album, *Greetings From Asbury Park, N.J.*, was completed. It was released in January, 1973. "I got a lot of things out in that first album," Bruce told a newsreporter, " . . . . a million things in each song. They were written in half-hour, fifteen minute blasts. I don't know where they came from . . . . I had all that stuff stored up for years."

Bruce had his first album with Columbia/CBS Records.

CHAPTER TWO

Born to run

Rock 'n' roll critics liked Bruce. They started calling him the "new Bob Dylan." Bruce was soon back in the recording studio making his second album, *The Wild, The Innocent and The E Street Shuffle*. It was released in early 1974. Bruce also continued to give concerts in cities all along the East coast. He started to experiment with special lighting and sound equipment. And he didn't just sing his songs. He started to tell a story before each song to help his audience understand them better. These stories were about his

A story about each song made his performance a powerful event.

life, his feelings, and his family. He was becoming a powerful performer.

Neither *Greetings From Asbury Park, N.J.* or *The Wild, The Innocent and The E Street Shuffle* sold very well. Columbia Records started to have second thoughts about Bruce doing a third album. Once again, Bruce needed help.

Jon Landau, a respected music critic for Boston's Real Paper, wrote, "I saw rock 'n' roll's future and its name is Bruce Springsteen." Bruce appreciated Landau's enthusiasm. "It gave me a lot of hope," he said, "The band and I were making fifty dollars a week. It helped me go on when I realized I was getting through to somebody." Landau's critical support also encouraged Columbia Records to let Bruce go into the studio and record his third album, *Born To Run*.

Bruce was under a lot of pressure. He needed to make an album that would sell well. And he needed one that radio stations all over the country would want to play. But he also wanted to take some chances on his newest record. A new sound—a bigger, more lush sound— was what he wanted to try for on *Born To Run*. He wanted to combine drums, cymbals, piano, organ, guitars, and saxophones with his singing. It was to be an ambitious rock 'n' roll effort.

The only problem was getting all of his ideas out of his head and onto the record. Bruce recalls, "I was unsure about the album all the way. I lost all perspective." During this time, Jon Landau had become

Bruce's friend. He helped Bruce make many important musical choices. He suggested that certain songs be cut down in length from seven minutes to three or four minutes. And he helped Bruce decide which instruments should be used and which ones should be featured alone in solo segments. But most important, Landau urged Bruce to keep working and finish *Born To Run*. Jon became the co-producer on the album and a long professional partnership began.

Rock 'n' roll fans and critics made *Born To Run* an instant success. It sold over a million copies the first year it was released. Bruce had not given up until he got the sound he wanted for his album. His determination and willingness to take risks had paid off.

A turning point

Released September 1, 1975, *Born To Run's* instant popularity with the record buying public meant Bruce suddenly started to get a lot of attention. On October 27, 1975, both Time and Newsweek featured Bruce Springsteen on their covers. Time called Bruce, "Rock's New Sensation." And Newsweek's headline read, "The Making of A Rock Star." No other rock 'n' roll musician had ever been singled out like this. Now, the entire country knew who Bruce was. He became famous overnight. He was no longer just a musician from Asbury Park, New Jersey. Time and Newsweek had declared him to be a rock 'n' roll "star."

Fame was quickly coming to Bruce.

There were many fans of rock 'n' roll, as well as some music critics, who did not feel Bruce deserved this kind of attention. Even Bruce wondered, ''What am I doing on the covers of Time and Newsweek? I'm not the President. I'm just a simple guy.'' Bruce wanted to make a name for himself, but he wanted to do it his way.

Also at this time, Bruce made his new friend, Jon Landau, his new manager. But Mike Appel, his original manager, fought this change. He filed a lawsuit against Bruce. Appel claimed that he owned all the songs Bruce had written. It took almost two years before Bruce regained ownership of his songs. During these two years, his legal problems with Appel kept him from recording any new songs.

It was a difficult period for Bruce. He couldn't make records, but he could perform in concert. But even this was not always easy for him. There was one night Bruce did not want to go on stage. It was the first time he had ever felt too low to sing. "At that moment," Bruce remembers, "I could see how people get into drinking or drugs, because the one thing you want at a time like that is to be distracted—in a big way."

But Bruce didn't turn to drinking or drugs. Instead he turned to his music. Music had always made him feel good about himself. And that's what he needed now.

Bruce asked himself, "What do I really want?" He discovered that what he really wanted was to be a "rocker, a musician—not a rock 'n' roll star."

Bruce wanted to be a musician.

CHAPTER THREE

Introducing the E Street Band

Bruce knew he needed great musicians to make great music. The E Street Band was first formed by Bruce in 1972. Bandmembers came and went for the next two years. But by 1974, Bruce had the musicians who would play with him for the next ten years.

The E Street Band is a rare rock 'n' roll group. All are very talented individuals who together create the special musical mixture Bruce needs behind him on stage or in the recording studio.

Clarence Clemons plays the saxophone. They call him "The Big Man" because he is. Before he joined Bruce's band, he played professional football. Clarence and Bruce have been friends a long time. Clarence played saxophone on Bruce's first album.

Danny Federici plays the organ, piano and the accordion. His nickname is "The Phantom." Like Clarence, Danny has known and worked with Bruce a long time. Danny first played with Bruce in 1968, when they played together in the band called Steel Mill.

Garry Tallent plays the bass guitar. And, as far as anyone knows, Garry does not have a nickname. He met Bruce in Asbury Park in the late 1960's. They played together in a band called Dr. Zoom and The Sonic Boom.

Roy Bittan plays keyboards. He studied music at Brooklyn College and everyone calls him the "Professor." He answered Bruce's ad in The Village Voice newspaper that read: "Drummer and keyboard player wanted for Bruce Springsteen and the E Street Band. Must sing." Roy made what he calls "the quickest phone call of my life." He auditioned and joined the E Street Band in 1974.

"Mighty" Max Weinberg is the drummer. He answered the same 1974 newspaper ad as Roy. He became a drummer because that was the only instrument available when he took music in school. He has played in rock 'n' roll bands since he was thirteen years old.

Steve Van Zandt plays the guitar and is known as "Miami" Steve. He is Bruce's closest friend. They grew up together in the Asbury Park area. "Miami" Steve has an interesting trademark—he never appears in public without a hat or scarf on his head. In 1984, he left Bruce to work with his own band, Little Steven and The Disciples of Soul. Nils Lofgren, veteran guitarist, replaced Van Zandt and is the latest addition to the E Street Band.

If you're a member of the band, you play by the rules.

Bruce becomes "The Boss"

Members of Bruce's band call him "The Boss." Bruce has certain rules. And if you are a member of the band, you play by the rules. You do not use drugs. You must be on time for rehearsals and performances. And you better be on the tour bus when it leaves town for the next concert date. Why? Because he's "The Boss."

The band goes to work

By 1977, Bruce's problems began to clear up. He had a new manager, Jon Landau. The lawsuits were

Bruce became a better musician and songwriter.

settled. Bruce could make records again. That's just what he did. Over the next five years, he made three albums: *Darkness At The Edge of Town* (1978), *The River* (1980), and *Nebraska* (1982). During these years, Bruce became a better musician and songwriter. He wrote more songs about his life and the things he knew about. Men and women losing their jobs, families that can't stay together, and people with broken hearts were a few of his themes. But not all his songs were sad. He also wrote music that made you want to get up and dance.

A work schedule started to develop. First, Bruce would make a record album. Then, after it was released, he and the E Street Band would travel to cities and give concerts.

With every new concert tour, Bruce started doing certain things that made his concerts different from other rock 'n' roll performers. For example, he did his own "sound checks." Sound checks happen before a performance. Sound experts usually go out into the middle of an empty auditorium and listen to the musicians on stage. But Bruce went one step further. He would listen from seats in the back row and seats off to the side of the stage. He listened from all over. He wanted to be sure each and every person in the audience would hear everything at that night's performance.

More practice, more work

Bruce wanted every show to be better than the last one. Once the show began, he was constantly moving. Bruce ran back and forth, up and down the entire stage. He jumped and slid around the floor; managing to sing and play his guitar at the same time. He dove into the audience's waiting arms, and then let them carry him back to the stage. He was everywhere. The energy he put into each show was tremendous. Springsteen concerts became known for their length. It was not unusual for him to stay on stage for three, or even four hours. He created a special event for his audiences. During a performance, he could easily lose three to five pounds of weight. That's how hard he worked.

The fans knew that Bruce had given them everything he had. Giving one hundred percent of himself was the only way Bruce knew how to perform. He liked to see his audiences go wild with excitement. That's what it was all about for him. For Bruce believes, ''that's the whole idea . . . . get excited . . . . do something . . . . be your own hero.''

Born in the USA

''You can make anything happen,'' Bruce tells his fans. And almost everything **did** happen for Bruce after

Good things began to happen after his album Born In The USA.

his album, *Born In The USA*, came out in June, 1984. It sold more copies than any of his other records. Fifteen million albums were sold in the United States and overseas. Rolling Stone magazine called *Born In The USA* one of the most popular albums in the last ten years.

Not everyone stayed home and listened to the album. A lot of fans were lucky enough to see him perform. The *Born In The USA* concert tour began in St. Paul, Minnesota on June 29, 1984, and would last almost one-and-one-half years. Bruce and the E Street Band played in sixty-one American cities and in seventeen foreign countries. When the tour ended, almost five million people had been to see "The Boss." According to some experts, it was perhaps the biggest concert tour in pop music history.

The years 1984 and 1985 were the biggest for Bruce. They were also his best. He painted powerful pictures with the words of his songs. *My Hometown*, *Glory Days*, and *Born In The USA* were a few of his new songs that told about the American spirit. From the concert stage, Bruce talked about Americans in trouble. He reminded his audiences that ". . . . in every city there are people going hungry. It's hard to believe it happens in a country so rich as ours."

But Bruce did more than talk about this problem. In every city that he played, he set up food banks. These are places where people can go and donate food or money. He set an example by giving one million dollars

of his own money to help feed the hungry and un-
employed.

"We Are
The World"

It was important for Bruce to help people in trouble.
Halfway through the *Born In The USA* tour, he took
time out to make a very special record called *We Are
The World*. The money earned from its record sales
would go to save the famine victims of Africa. Bruce
knew he wanted to be involved with the making of this
record.

On the night of January 28, 1985, over forty
American pop and rock stars gathered at a Hollywood
recording studio. Bruce joined such stars as Lionel

*Willie Nelson and Bruce Springsteen (right) are pictured
during the rehearsal of* We Are The World.

27

Richie, Tina Turner, Michael Jackson, Bob Dylan, Cyndi Lauper and many more. They had only this one night to learn the song and to get it recorded. It was a unique evening. So much talent in one room and everyone working together for one goal—to save lives.

Bruce had done a four hour show the night before in Syracuse, New York. He had flown all day to make

Bruce had done a four hour show the night before.

this recording session in California. Everyone worked through the night and into the early morning hours of the next day. By the time Bruce recorded his solo part of *We Are The World*, it was after five o'clock in the morning. He was tired, but not too tired to give it his best. As he stepped up to the microphone, he called to a departing Bob Dylan, "you sounded fantastic." When Bruce first started performing, Dylan was the man most people said he sounded like. But when Bruce began to sing that night, it was clear his sound was all his own.

Putting the sheet music in his back pocket, he told Quincy Jones, the conductor, he was ready. "I'll give it a shot," Bruce said. He sang his solo part perfectly the first time. The sun had come up when Bruce left the recording studio. He had given his time and talent to make *We Are The World* a success.

This time success would be measured not just by record sales, but by the number of lives saved from starvation. *We Are The World* earned almost fifty million dollars (US) in one year. And at the 1986 Grammy Awards Ceremony, it won a Grammy for Best Record. This is the highest honor the music business gives to artists and their work. Other fund raising events followed the example set by the *We Are The World* artists. The Live Aid concert in July, 1985, and the Farm Aid concert in September, 1985, were organized to help Africans and Americans in need.

Mr. and Mrs. Springsteen

Bruce certainly worked hard, but he did find time to fall in love. Julianne Phillips came into Bruce's life during the *Born In The USA* tour. They met in Los Angeles when Julianne went backstage after one of his shows. He knew she was special the moment they met. Bruce had had many girlfriends before meeting Julianne. But music had always come first with him. He didn't think that he would ever settle down and get married.

Six months after they met, Bruce and Julianne decided to get married in her hometown of Lake Oswego, Oregon. They wanted to have a private ceremony with

Bruce Springsteen and actress Julianne Phillips were married in May, 1985.

only their family and friends around them. It was tough to keep it a secret. As soon as news of the wedding leaked out, all sorts of things started to happen in Lake Oswego. The local radio station set up a "Springsteen rumor hotline." Fans, reporters, and photographers began camping out in front of Julianne's parents' home. One determined young man even promised to mow a neighbor's lawn for a year, if she would go next door and get Bruce's autograph for him.

Luckily, reporters and fans never found out that the wedding date had been moved up three days. Bruce and Julianne would be married as soon as their marriage license permitted it. Shortly after midnight on Monday, May 13, 1985, they arrived at the church. The only

other people there were the family and friends, about fifty-five people, that they had invited. Bruce and Julianne got their wish. Their wedding was quiet and beautiful.

When the *Born In The USA* tour ended in Los Angeles in October, 1985, Bruce had a beautiful wife, a successful concert tour, and one of the most popular record albums ever recorded. It was a very good year. And Bruce knew it. He closed his last show with, "It's been the greatest year of my life. And I want to thank you for making me feel like the luckiest man in the world."

1985 was the best year in Bruce's life.